RAGE OR REASON

THE ECONOMIC AND POLITICAL CHOICES
FACED BY MILLENNIALS

VINCENT H. L. MICHAELS

Copyright © 2020 Vincent H. L. Michaels.

All rights reserved. The information in this book was correct at the time of publication, but the author does not assume any liability for loss or damage caused by errors or omissions. Author has made every effort to contact all copyright holders.

ISBN: 978-1-7325347-9-7

First paperback edition October 2020

Publish Authority
300 Colonial Center Parkway, Suite 100
Roswell, GA 30076

www.PublishAuthority.com

CONTENTS

Preface	vii
Chapter 1 *A Complex Theory For A Complex World*	1
Chapter 2 *Free-market Economy and Socialism*	5
Chapter 3 *Economic Inequalities*	9
Chapter 4 *Socialism, Like In The Scandinavian Countries*	12
Chapter 5 *Collectivism, Individualism, And Guns*	14
Chapter 6 *It Will Be All Free*	17
Chapter 7 *Concerning Medicare-For-All*	20
Chapter 8 *Globalization And Nation-States*	24
Chapter 9 *Diversity*	26
Chapter 10 *About Climate Change*	29
Chapter 11 *Logical Fallacies Used As Logical Proofs*	33
Chapter 12 *How Some Politicians Enrich Themselves While In Office*	36
Afterword	39
Acknowledgments	41
References	43

To the patriot: Freedom and Liberty

PREFACE

It is an attribute of youth to be passionate. Many US young Millennials fight for causes they find worthwhile, and many of them are captivated by the grandiose projects of the progressive Left to "save Humanity" such as "Climate Change" or "The Green New Deal". They feel they have enough knowledge and wisdom to decide if a cause is worth their time and involvement or not.

They forget, or are unaware that, several years back, other similar youths of the progressive Left of the time were having a similar enthusiasm for other grandiose projects to "save Humanity":

In 1918, just after the Bolsheviks' Revolution in Russia, the newborn Soviet Socialist Republic decided they would improve agriculture (mostly cotton) by fertilizing the desert surrounding the Aral Sea, a large inland body of water East of the Caspian Sea. As it is today, the science was then certain and nothing could go wrong. This resulted in one of the worst man-made ecological disasters of all time[1]. By diverting fresh water from its feeding rivers, the Aral Sea progressively dried up, most of it turning into a desert. While the cotton industry soared, the fishing industry collapsed. This dry new desert also started producing dust storms carrying the chemicals and pesticides previously dumped into the sea hundreds of miles away. The ensuing pollution created many health hazards in the area such as cancer, liver and kidney damages, etc.

In 1958, other enthusiastic leftists who were members of the Chinese communist party also contemplated another grandiose project called "The Great Leap Forward" to modernize both industry and agriculture in China[2]. As is being done today by the Left, critics were shamed or "canceled". The Great Leap Forward resulted in "The Great Chinese Famine" with between 18 to 45 million deaths —the worst famine in our history[3].

It easy to be seduced by the siren's songs of the progressive Left. They are so certain of their science and philosophy, and their projects and ideas sound so good and well thought that they forget that the most valid law of human behavior is that of unintended consequences and that the road to hell is paved with good intentions. The grand projects of the current progressive Left seem foolproof in their logic. Yet, there are significant flaws in their argumentation that this book tries to bring to light.

Then, the main goal of the Left's (and now also the Democrats') grandiose projects usually seems to reduce itself to moving money around. This allows the Left and Democrat politicians to get their cut in one way or the other. All (or nearly all) Democrat and Leftist politicians end up wealthy despite their meager government salaries. How do you think this happens?

Rage or Reason tries to not only bring attention to some facts and arguments not mentioned by the Left, but also to uncover the ulterior financial motives of their grandiose "Save the World" projects and ideas as well as the mechanisms allowing their politicians to get rich from them.

It is hoped that this short book will help the younger generation make a more informed opinion before dedicating themselves to a cause. It is also hoped that it will provide valuable arguments for non-Left individuals when debating with their Leftist counterparts.

CHAPTER 1

A COMPLEX THEORY FOR A COMPLEX WORLD

TODAY'S WORLD IS COMPLICATED, especially when you consider its societal, political, and economic constituents. Some other aspects of our world also require an understanding of the underlying sciences, climate change being a prime example of such. Unfortunately, many people examine current issues with the lens of yesterday's knowledge, without using all the analytic tools currently available.

Complexity theory is such a tool, and it is necessary to understand some important aspects of current issues that are not otherwise obvious. This theory is especially important when it comes to economic inequalities and climate change, which will be discussed in later chapters. It is important to at least have a basic knowledge of it.

The modern science of complex systems (complexity theory) has surprisingly simple implications:

1. A system is deemed complex if it has many interdependent and interacting parts.

2. Complex systems are totally unpredictable, even if one uses simulations with supercomputers or even quantum computers. *For example, economic computer programs (substantially similar to the programs used for climate) foresaw or predicted neither the financial crisis of 2008 nor the economic repercussions of the unexpected current coronavirus pandemic (2020).*
3. Their changes in outcomes often follow a probability curve resembling a Bell's curve, but with "fat tails" (the top (red) curve at both the left and right extremes of the x-axis in Figure 1).

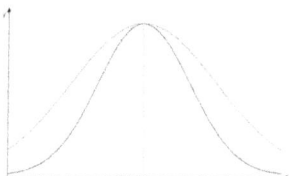

Figure 1: Bell probability curve (bottom) and complex probability curve (top).

IN THE BELL PROBABILITY CURVE and complex probability curve (Figure 1), the x-axis represents a variable (increasing average Earth temperature from left to right, for example). The y-axis represents the frequency of occurrence. The bottom (black) line represents an ordinary Bell curve. The top (red) line has the "fat tails" of complex systems at both ends, meaning that rare events at the extreme left and right are more frequent. The vertical (green) line represents the mean. In this example, the chance of a much warmer climate 20 years out is the same as the chance of a much colder one.

Events that occur at both extremes of the x-axis are called "Black Swan Events"[4]. They are rarer than the number of events seen near the mean of the curve but more frequent than if they were due to chance alone (Bell's curve, drawn in black).

This means that events at both extremes of the probability curve are more frequent than what would be seen if they were due to chance alone.

4. They are associated with power laws[5] ⋯(Figure 2).

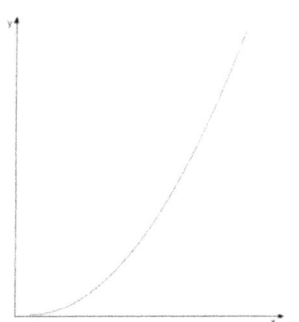

Figure 2: A power law curve.

IN THE POWER LAW CURVE (Figure 2), the y-axis could represent the frequency distribution of letters in the alphabet (from z, q ...to ... e, along the x-axis), the frequency distribution of words in any language, the population ranks of US cities or the frequency distribution of income or wealth among the various percentiles of the population (themselves represented along the x-axis). All are complex systems, which follow similar power laws.

Power laws are intimately associated with complex systems, which frequently manifest through them. Complex economies must self-organize into hierarchical structures in order to function[6]. For example, a few large financial institutions move tremendously large amounts of money; a larger number of smaller institutions move smaller amounts and, at the other end of the curve, a very large number of individuals move relatively much smaller amounts.

CHAPTER 2
FREE-MARKET ECONOMY AND SOCIALISM

SOCIALISM PROMOTES the concept of equal distribution of wealth and income among all people. It is based on Karl Marx's analysis of 19th-century capitalism (a name given to the free-market economy at the time), and concludes that capitalists *inherently* exploit workers[7].

However, a key flaw in Marx's analysis is that he only analyzed successful businesses. He did not take into consideration all the entrepreneurs who try to start a business but fail. In modern behavioral economics terms, this would be called a "survivorship bias."

Now, if you would, add to the group of successful businesses the much more numerous capitalist entrepreneurs who fail and become deeply in debt (often with personal loan guarantees), the money lost by the latter group at least partially balances out the money gained by the former. On the other hand, workers get to keep their incomes and don't share the entrepreneurs' losses and debts.

One, therefore, cannot conclude that capitalism *inherently* exploits labor.

Marx had predicted that the workers living conditions would deteriorate as their pay decreases to the minimum needed to survive. On the contrary, their standard of living and pay improved over time. Vladimir Lenin (who led the successful Russian communist revolution of 1917) tried to explain this discrepancy. Lenin argued that rich capitalist countries were now exploiting third world nations through imperialism (a type of financial and economic control of developing nations without necessarily occupying them as in colonialism), allowing these rich countries to pay their workers better[8]. If this was true, capitalism should have collapsed once former colonies won their independence and changed their economies to seek their own best interests. Again, the opposite occurred, and capitalism continued to thrive.

Socialist theoreticians have invoked all kinds of reasons why the free-market economies have been so resilient. Contemporary leftist thinkers have focused on economic inequalities presumably brought about by the free-market system[9, 10]. This will be the subject of our next chapter.

Socialism is better described as "bureaucratic parasitism." In order to reward its supporters with jobs, socialism must create a large bureaucracy. As a result, this large but necessary-to-socialism bureaucracy is unable to create, or generate, wealth and functions at the expense of those who do, therefore the endemic poverty seen in socialist countries.

It is important to understand that socialism cannot create wealth because its managers are inherently risk-averse: no one wants the stigma of failure and not be promoted in the socialist bureaucratic hierarchy. Behavioral economics has shown that people fear failure more than they love success. If a socialist bureaucrat risks but fails, she/he could face career dampening or career-ending repercussions. Only capitalist economies provide sufficient rewards for those willing to take risks.

Another reason why capitalism creates wealth where socialism does not is that it self-organizes efficiently near its lowest costs, something that the bloated socialist bureaucracies cannot do. Capitalism also rewards those who know how to create wealth. Conversely, socialism only rewards those who know how to be good socialists. More often than not, socialist bureaucrats have no clue on how to create wealth.

We now know that socialism does not work in practice, not because it is a valid political theory that has been poorly applied, but because socialist theory is deeply and irreversibly flawed at its core. This is the ultimate reason why it does not work.

Since Marx, there has been a tremendous amount of leftist literature explaining why capitalism is bad, some using very complicated and convoluted arguments.

But capitalists make money by **selling** products or services. They, therefore, have a strong incentive to see everyone wealthy enough to buy what they sell.

Exploiting workers would only bring the capitalist a pittance in profits compared to making sure workers (as a group) are well enough financially to become customers. The same applies to developing nations. Capitalists get wealthier by everyone else becoming sufficiently wealthy. This is what has been seen in practice.

CHAPTER 3
ECONOMIC INEQUALITIES

"ECONOMIC INEQUALITY" is a rallying cry of the Left[9, 10], and is a reason given by leftists to promote socialism. They see inequalities of wealth and income as the cause of all evils. Socialism, they say, will distribute wealth equally among all members of society and cure all social ills.

In socialist economies, marked inequalities do exist. However, they do not manifest as differences in wealth or income but as differences in the degree of perks and privileges one gets in the socialist hierarchy, resulting in large inequities in the living standards of the populace.

For example, a mid-level bureaucrat of the communist party of the former USSR would be provided with a large mansion in an upscale neighborhood, a car with a driver, as well as servants and cooks. She/he would also have access to goods and services not available to the general public (for example, a parallel and much better health care system)[11]. If we translate or compare the perks and privileges of the socialist elites to their free-market equivalents, we actually see much worse inequalities than those that exist in capitalist countries.

Economic inequalities are not due to the nature of the economy (capitalist, socialist, or other). Significant inequalities occur in ALL advanced economies irrespective of their nature. Economic inequalities are due to the fact that economies are *complex*.

As we have seen, complexity expresses itself by power laws (Fig. 2). These power laws manifest as inequalities (the difference between the y-axis values at each end of the red (gray) curve of Figure 2). All complex systems exhibit such behavior, and it cannot be avoided[5].

For example, the most frequent letter of the English alphabet ("e") occurs about 12% of the time in a given text while the least frequent (usually "z", or "q" depending on the study used) occurs only 0.07% of the time, a marked difference in the frequency of occurrence.

Sophisticated and complex products and services, such as cellular phones, Internet, spaceships, etc., can only be produced by a sophisticated and *complex economy*. This complex economy cannot be dissociated from its specific *power laws and their implied inequalities*. These factors are interdependent and cannot be separated[5, 6]:

SOPHISTICATED PRODUCTS and
SERVICES = COMPLEXITY =
POWER LAWS = INEQUALITIES

IMAGINE HOW DIFFICULT IT WOULD BE TO USE the English language if you had to use each word with the same frequency of occurrence.

Also, imagine how difficult it would be to write if you had to use all letters with the same frequency of occurrence.

If our population was obliged to be distributed evenly across the country, we would not be able to have a sufficient concentration of individuals to build large airports or factories, and the world would look very different. It would look like it did when the only people around were small groups of hunter-gatherers. The hunter-gatherer economy was the only economy that had some semblance of equality. Still, they would never have been able to provide the degree of technology we have now become accustomed to expect.

Because capitalism efficiently creates wealth, it is able to lift the lower part of its power law curve much more efficiently than socialism. It has therefore been more efficient at lifting people out of poverty over time than has socialism.

Some may claim that inequalities are inherently unfair, but they are not more inherently unfair than the fact that some people get sick while others do not. Inequalities are necessary for the adequate functioning of any sophisticated economy providing modern services and products.

CHAPTER 4

SOCIALISM, LIKE IN THE SCANDINAVIAN COUNTRIES

THE SCANDINAVIAN COUNTRIES are not socialist; they have capitalist economies with wide social safety nets. Politically, they are, for the most part, parliamentary constitutional monarchies[12].

Their social safety nets work because they are relatively wealthy and not very populated. The most populous of them is Sweden, with about 10 million individuals, while the US population is about 327 million at the time of this writing[12].

There are also significant differences in tradition and culture. In Nordic countries with socialized medicine (the equivalent of "Medicare-for-All"), people have to wait twice as long—on average—to get medical treatment than in the US.

Higher education may also be "free" in Nordic countries ("free" in the sense that it is funded by taxes), but there is a drastic selection process based only on test grades. Those who make it through this grading process are few, which is why higher education remains affordable. In the US, the Left wants everyone to get a free college degree, which is an entirely different approach and an exponentially more expensive proposition.

The Scandinavian population has also remained relatively homogeneous (i.e., Nordic Caucasians) until recently, while the US population has a much more diverse history.

The liberal Left keeps making the mistake of thinking that you can proportionately extrapolate the Scandinavian models of education and socialized health care to the US. The much larger and more diverse population of the United States adds many layers of complexity to the organization of higher education and health care.

Bottom line: What works for Scandinavia would not necessarily work for the US. We have to find our own original solutions.

CHAPTER 5

COLLECTIVISM, INDIVIDUALISM, AND GUNS

SOCIALISM IS the economic manifestation of *collectivism*, a philosophy that assumes all people are always equal in every way and must be rewarded equally—whether they merit it or not. Collectivism, AKA socialism, gives precedence to the group over the individual. On the other hand, *individualism* favors the person, the individual, over the group.

This collective-individual duality is best illustrated by considering the gun issue: If you look at the statistics, there are at least as many people saved by the use of a gun as killed by it (yet, the liberal Left acknowledges only the latter)[13]. Many collectivist countries, such as those in Western Europe (the UK, for example), make it very difficult to use a gun for self-defense, even against violent aggression. If a criminal enters your house at night, how do you know whether this individual is armed or not? Yet, if you shoot an unarmed intruder, you're much more likely (than in the US) to face criminal charges and possibly do time. If the intruder is armed and ill-intentioned, you might end up dead if you hesitate.

Individualistic philosophy allows you to be armed for personal self-defense, the protection of your family, close ones, and your property. Individualistically oriented laws also favor you over an eventual aggressor.

In practice, law enforcement officers will seldom arrive at a scene in time to stop a crime. If attacked, your ultimate line of defense is still a gun to ward off the aggressor, and the simple view of it might be sufficient to dissuade the individual from proceeding further.

The Federalist Papers, along with the Second Amendment of the US Constitution, make it clear that the Founding Fathers wanted an armed population as a last-ditch defense against tyranny[14, 15]. If you think tyranny could not happen in the United States, think again. Venezuela used to be a wealthy capitalist country not so long ago. In fact, in 1950, Venezuela was the world's 4th ***wealthiest*** nation per capita, but since 1992 it has devolved into socialism with a de-facto dictator and is now recognized as a "Failed State." By some measures, it is even considered the world's worst-performing economy[16]. One of the first things done by dictators is to ban private gun ownership, which the Chavez government indeed did in 2012.

Do you want to be the sacrificial offering on the altar of collectivism? Individualism puts you first, where the state is a servant of each of its citizens and where its laws defend you against criminals.

Collectivism, on the other hand, does not put you first. Although you're theoretically allowed to defend yourself and your family in collectivist countries, the use of a firearm will almost certainly result in you facing criminal prosecution and possible jail time, especially if it is to protect property[17]. If the homicide rate is indeed lower in most European countries compared to the US, theft, robbery, and kidnapping rates are higher in many of these countries[18,19].

CHAPTER 6
IT WILL BE ALL FREE

WHEN A PRODUCT or service is free, it means that you, yourself, are the real product being traded. Fishermen use bait, which is "free" food for the fishes they try to catch. Politicians do the same with "freebies." Freebies are bait for the unwary.

When Democrats, Progressives, or any other politicians promise you "free stuff" (whatever it is), you can be certain that this "free stuff" is bait. In taking that bait, you get trapped in an addiction to freebies—not realizing that your personal freedom is being compromised or restrained. Your mind is being molded by selective and often biased and misleading information so that you attain a level of group-think and become a minion among the collective of progressive minions. Then, your primary purpose to the liberal Left's leaders is to keep them in power for their socialist utopia.

Like a leech sucks the blood of its host, the socialist parasitic bureaucracy sucks all available products and services out of its country's economy, and nothing remains for the minions who took the bait. The media will not remind you of the long cue lines with people waiting for hours sometimes to get a simple piece of bread in that former socialist experiment of the Union of Soviet Socialist Republics (the USSR, commonly referred to as the Soviet Union). And now we see this experience repeated in modern-day Venezuela among other socialist countries. They also will not remind you of the famines that killed tens of millions of people in Ukraine (then part of the Soviet Union) and communist China at the time of Mao Zedong[3].

And when every minion becomes a socialist bureaucrat scrambling to finally get her or his fair share of the socialist utopia, the system collapses from its own weight and inertia. This scenario has now played out in the real world so often that it would become boring if it were not so tragic (again, Venezuela is the latest example, but there are many others).

The only instances where socialist regimes have done better is when they have enacted enough free-market reforms to actually create wealth (China, for example). But do not underestimate the voracious appetite of the socialist bureaucracy. Sooner or later, it will require all the wealth of its country to support itself and pay for the perks and privileges of its elites.

A real and effective free-market economy needs freedom of thought to innovate and thrive. Alas, freedom of thought and socialism are not compatible. For example, China has recently made it illegal to question the tenets of socialism. Similarly, in the US, the socialist Left has put the "woke and cancel" culture in place to silence our freedom of speech. Do not expect the free-market reforms of socialist countries and their consequent economic improvements to last in the long run.

CHAPTER 7

CONCERNING MEDICARE-FOR-ALL

IT IS SAID that the US spends more than anyone else in the world for less quality healthcare[20]. The US average healthcare cost per capita is indeed about twice its counterpart in the Nordic countries that have a nationalized healthcare system (the Medicare-for-All equivalent). When one takes into consideration the different ways the data is collected, the various definitions for outcomes, etc., the quality of care is actually about the same for all advanced economies. This would be expected considering the rapid diffusion of health information through journals, meetings, the Internet, etc.

What is also different is that you get treatment much faster in the US than in these Nordic countries[21]. People in the US are therefore paying for faster service. It's like the difference in price between overnight delivery and regular mail.

It is quite a problem not to have enough money to get appropriate medical care. Still, money is emotionless: it might be an even more difficult problem to have to deal with a stubborn bureaucrat (and

Medicare-for-All would require a lot of bureaucracy). For example, the United Kingdom (UK) has a nationalized healthcare system similar to the Medicare-for-All system that progressives want in the US. Do you remember that baby Alfie Evans in the UK? Alfie was a 23-month-old boy who died in 2018 from a rare genetic disease. The UK doctors and the UK government agents proclaimed everyone with that condition has always died and declared that any treatment for baby Alfie would be futile[22]. Therefore, they would not allow the parents to pursue further medical treatment for their baby boy, including taking their child to the US to attempt an experimental treatment that might have saved his life. However, there had only been (about) 26 other such cases in the world, which is not a large enough number for UK doctors and government agents to make such a statistical extrapolation. Perhaps, Alfie would have been the first successful case if given the treatment that was being considered.

Alfie's case is yet one more example of what can go wrong when bureaucrats make decisions for you (healthcare decisions, in this case). Bureaucratic "Death Panels" such as this decide when you or your loved ones might be allowed to be medically treated or not, and when it might just be cheaper for the state to let you die.

Of western countries with a bona fide nationalized healthcare system, the UK is the most populated at about 65 million[12]. Complexity significantly increases with a larger population, and a model that works for 65 million would not necessarily work for 327 million. By and large, true and fair competitive capitalism is best at minimizing inefficiencies while large socialist bureaucracies are best at maximizing them. The best system for the US will end up being a free-market one.

Healthcare is meant to treat real diseases, not normal conditions perceived by the Left as diseases such as pregnancy and gender. It does not appear normal that public money should be used for medical or surgical procedures related to these conditions as this money would then be unavailable to improve care for real pathologies such as cancer or cardiac research.

With new technologies and treatments that allow us to cure more diseases, healthcare has become expensive. Meanwhile, there is not an unlimited amount of dollars to dedicate to it. Expanding healthcare coverage to all those who illegally enter the country dilutes what is available for legal immigrants and citizens.

Currently, in the US, illegal immigrants also often clog acute care facilities, which are not always allowed to transfer them to chronic care hospitals. Consequently, these facilities' rooms are then not available to patients who might be in more need of them.

The current US healthcare system may have issues and inefficiencies that need to be solved. Still, when compared to the socialized Medicare-for-All systems, it has the advantages of 1. being faster, and 2. letting you make your healthcare decisions.

For your own sake, you certainly do not want a bureaucrat to be making healthcare decisions for you. The freebies of socialized medicine will sound nice until you have to wait forever to get appropriate medical care. Or, until you're told by a healthcare bureaucrat that you're too old (or too sick or any other reason—as in Alfie's case) for that care anyway.

CHAPTER 8

GLOBALIZATION AND NATION-STATES

GLOBALIZATION REPRESENTS for nations what socialism represents for individuals. The globalists want to revive the concept of a world empire. But all the empires of history have divided into individual *nation-states* with their distinctive cultures and languages: for example, in the Western European empire of Charlemagne[23] and in the Eastern empire of Genghis Khan (which covered the territory from Eastern Russia to China)[24]. Small states and city-states have themselves coalesced into *nation-states* over time, for example, Greece[25] and Italy[26].

For the foreseeable future, it appears that the *nation-state* will remain the most viable political and geographical entity.

In as much as you want a representative government enacting laws that you will follow, there must be a geographical line of demarcation as to where these laws cease to apply and other laws from other representative governments start being applied. Therefore, borders—and by the same token, nation-states—are necessities for governments and laws to be meaningful.

CHAPTER 9

DIVERSITY

WE ALL WOULD PREFER to live in an all-inclusive society, without prejudice or racism.

Since the "affirmative action" Executive Order of 1961, there has been an effort by the US government to promote racial diversity as a way to curtail racism. This has been meant to give minority racial groups better access to education and jobs where they previously had been shunned because of bias. To achieve these goals, forced quotas have been imposed on academia and business by the government.

However, diversity by forced quota has not-infrequently resulted in the promotion of individuals solely chosen on the basis of race, without enough concern as to their qualifications. So, instead of having a promotion/admission system based on merit alone (the only fair system), one racial favoritism (e.g., favoring Caucasians) was simply replaced by another (e.g., favoring African Americans).

This role reversal may appear to some as poetic justice, but it has the effect of exacerbating prejudice and racism instead of eliminating it. Indeed, racial favoritism carries within it the insidious implication (deserved or not) that individuals benefiting from it are unable to get their positions on their own merit. It also seems unfair to throw unprepared students into academia when they are not ready for the workload and rigors necessary to confront stringent testing requirements.

What the Left wants is not to eliminate racial bias but to reverse it. By the Left's discriminative legislation, not only are selected minority racial groups (mainly African Americans) to be given preference when individuals have equal merit and qualifications, they must also be given preference even when less meritorious or qualified than their non-African-American counterparts. Promoting racial bias, even in a reverse fashion, is certainly not going to improve racism. It will worsen it.

Fairness is an important concept for Americans (and for the efficient functioning of the free-market economy). In general, Americans feel that everyone should have an equal chance of success. Success based on merit is also more admired than success based on luck or skin color.

The best way to remedy racial discrepancies is to maintain a totally blind merit-based system for promotions and hiring. Give individuals coveting a certain position a given amount of relevant material to study, a given time to study it, and promote (hire/accept/...) the one person with the best score (use a second harder test to differentiate equal scores or simply roll a dice). Despite its shortcomings, it is quite possible that even subtle aspects of racism would rapidly be weeded out with such a system.

Promoting unmeritorious individuals does not do them any favors as they have to face the task of making appropriate decisions or look incompetent, something that can have great repercussions on their careers and self-esteem. It is much better to appropriately train and educate these individuals in the first place. In the example of African Americans, there is no reason it should not be so. Thomas Sowell, in his recent book about charter schools, has shown that African-American kids can do even better than their non-minorities peers under the appropriate circumstances[27].

CHAPTER 10
ABOUT CLIMATE CHANGE

THE DEMOCRATS and the liberal Left predict a soon-to-happen-end-of-the-world due to out of control global warming of the planet. This global warming (also called climate change) is presumably due to the carbon dioxide created by our use of fossil fuels. Of course, they argue that large sums of money (US *taxpayers'* money) are needed to combat this. Fighting climate change was codified in an international agreement called "The Paris Accord", signed in 2015[28].

Many countries were glad to subscribe to this "Accord" because they were promised these funds. Considering the corruption prevalent in so many countries[29, 30], you can be certain that this money would never have been used to actually fight climate change, but would have ended up in the private tax heavens' bank accounts of corrupt politicians, their families and cronies.

There are also many shortcomings in the Climate Change theory:

1. Climate may be simpler than Weather,

but it is still a complex system[5]. As such, it is not predictable, even with models generated by supercomputers or even quantum computers. Ten, twenty years from now, the climate has the same probability of being colder than of being warmer according to the curve of Figure 1 (consider the fact that without the so maligned greenhouse effect of the atmosphere, the sun can only warm the planet to about 0°F or -18°C[31]. The claim of some youths that their future has been "stolen" from them may be emotionally appealing, but it is false. No one can steal a future that cannot be accurately predicted.

2. All temperature measurements before very recent times have been reconstructed by indirect methods, each with its own set of uncertainties. Climate science can, therefore, only be a probabilistic theory, never a certainty.

3. We are currently in the warm interglacial period of a 100,000-150,000 years climate cycle. Scientifically, this cannot be due to the human use of fossil fuels[32, 33].

4. Atmospheric CO_2 has also been much higher in the far past than it is today, and this didn't destroy life on Earth[33, 34]. There is also evidence that decreasing CO_2 levels may have resulted in deforestation and subsequent loss of animal species (as

trees need more CO_2 than grasses)[35]. Also, the amount of CO_2 produced by volcanic and hydrothermal activity is currently considered to be a fraction of that produced by fossil fuels. But it is largely unknown how much such activity actually occurs under the oceans today. The estimates might be way off, and some even argue that an increase in atmospheric CO_2 might be beneficial[36].

5. The often-seen-on-TV melting of Antarctica's ice-sheets appears to be mostly due to sub-ice volcanic activity rather than to global warming, as the areas of ice melting coincide with the areas of such activity[37].

At this moment, there are still too many uncertainties about Climate Change to consider it an established scientific truth. Most of the Left's arguments about climate change are based on *long-term projections* from sophisticated computer models. However, we have seen that climate, as all complex systems, cannot be predicted.

Scientists should know better than believe that feeding data to a supercomputer would allow them to predict the future. Remember that similar computer models have been developed for the economy and that they spectacularly failed to predict the economic collapse of 2008 or the economic effects of the 2020 coronavirus pandemic. This should have taught some humility to the climate change scientists, but it's obviously not the case.

Even if one believes in atmospheric CO_2 driven climate warming, they should take their case to China and other emerging economies which contribute a whopping 55% of all estimated CO_2 emissions (29% for China alone). In comparison, the US contributes only 16%.

CHAPTER 11

LOGICAL FALLACIES USED AS LOGICAL PROOFS

THE MEDIA and the Left are presenting logical fallacies as if they were logical proofs. Progressive journalists routinely use these types of logical substitutions, and this has recently become more frequent.

Fallacies are mistaken beliefs based on invalid arguments that have been made persuasive artificially. Here are a few examples:

FALLACY OF HASTY GENERALIZATION

This fallacy appears to be the most frequent: in order to come to a valid answer to a statistical question, one must use a valid statistical sample, and a limited number of examples do not represent such a sample. For example, claiming that a person is racist toward "green people" because she/he does not like a few specific members of that group is an invalid argument.

FALLACY OF EMOTIONAL APPEAL

An appeal to emotions (pity, indignation, anger, etc...) is used in an attempt to suspend one's ability to think critically. Accepting such an appeal results in accepting an otherwise invalid claim. For example, the skewed charge that the US government is inhumanly separating illegal immigrant families at the US southern border is being used by the Left to create indignation, which is then used to persuade people that illegal immigration should be tolerated.

However, any person convicted and jailed will also be separated from her/his family, and so would people who work far from home, for example, a sailor going on a tour of duty.

It must be said that a majority of the children of the illegal immigrant "families" seen at the southern US border are not at all family members but unrelated children taken along for purpose of human trafficking or to be used as shields.

Moreover, there are many good reasons to control immigration into the US. Confining the spread of infectious diseases is one example: antibiotic-resistant tuberculosis is endemic to Central America[38], and no one should want it to spread in the US. The same is true for the coronavirus pandemic, open borders are a call to spread the infection.

FALLACY OF "TRUTH FROM THE CROWD"

This fallacy claims that something is true because a crowd (meaning a large number of people) say it is. Lately, it has been heard mostly in the context of climate change. For example, claiming again and again that many or most climate "experts" believe that the future of climate can be predicted with computer models does not make it true. We have seen that climate, as all other complex systems, is unpredictable.

The above are a few of the frequent fallacies being purported as mainstream truths today. There are others, and the reader is encouraged to study them[39]. Detecting false arguments such as these "Truth-from-the-Crowd" arguments is a great strength, and so is one's ability to construct a logically sound argument to counter falsehoods.

CHAPTER 12

HOW SOME POLITICIANS ENRICH THEMSELVES WHILE IN OFFICE

SOCIALISM, income inequality, globalization, diversity, and climate change: these are some of the unproven grandiose socialist theories that the Left and the Democrats use to make your money their money.

Their strategy goes as follows:

1. Find some grandiose issue with strong emotional appeal.
2. Use that issue as an excuse to tax the populace.
3. Move this tax money from those who earned it to those who didn't: the politicians' family members, supporters, cronies, and friends, using businesses and organizations that will presumably "solve" the issues. Usually, nothing is actually solved; the new businesses rapidly collapse because the individuals involved have no clue on how to create wealth, but not before they fill their

own pockets with the subsidies provided by US tax dollars. Remember President Obama's $80 billion solar-panel company Solyndra boondoggle[40].

4. The politician or high-ranking government official involved also makes sure that part of this money is recycled toward him or her in one fashion or the other (political contributions, votes, money contributions to a foundation, etc.). For example, some of the US government's subsidies, grants or aid to foreign governments or non-governmental organizations (NGOs) often end up in the hands of corrupt foreign politicians or individuals without ever making it to its intended recipients or causes. These funds are instead rerouted to the corrupt US politicians or political parties and their various associates[41].

These under-the-table maneuvers are not exclusive to the progressives and democrats. Some republicans-in-name-only (RINOs) and other corrupt politicians or government officials are also guilty as charged[42].

If the democrats and Left win, they will invite all their friends, family, cronies, and supporters to become bureaucrats in the new socialist bureaucracy. This socialist bureaucratic parasite will then get larger at the expense of the rest of the population until it collapses under its own weight as already addressed in this short treatise. This political scenario is the fulfilled utopia of what is called "Democratic Socialism".

AFTERWORD

We have seen that the socialist/progressive ideology has many flaws, as well as a poor understanding that the most established law of human behavior is that of unintended consequences.

The Marxist theory underpinning socialism has a flaw of survivorship bias. Collectivism might appear to be appealing until you are the one sacrificed on its altars. The progressive/leftist views on inequalities and climate have flaws due to their poor understanding of how complex systems actually behave.

The progressives and the Left have either a poor knowledge of history or poor memory or both. They forget that, in their time, other leftists and progressives dreamed of grandiose projects (equivalent to the Green New Deal or the Climate Change Theory) that were also going to save mankind. However, when actually implemented in the real world, these programs or projects only led to disasters. The Aral Sea ecological fiasco[1] and the Great Chinese Famine[2, 3] are such examples. There are others.

Even Thomas Piketty, probably one of the most influential contemporary progressive thinker and writer, acknowledges that the communist experience was a failure[43]. Incredibly, however, he still advocates such large-scale social experimentation where previous experiences have shown that unintended consequences have been the most prevalent outcome.

Despite its previous failures, socialism and leftist ideologies are once again regurgitated to the people in a new palatable disguise for the purpose of yet another insidious attempt to gain power. This "late-stage-socialism" and its leftists' unproven or misconceived ideas are no better than their "brethren" of the two past centuries. They do not represent the future of our country.

Only a fair and merit-based free-market economy will have enough power and momentum to propel us through the new millennium.

We expect the reader to research further the various topics covered rather than non-critically accept the progressive Left's narrative. If such is the case, then these few pages will have achieved their purpose.

ACKNOWLEDGMENTS

I am especially indebted to Publish Authority for its help preparing this book and making it a reality.

Frank Eastland, from Publish Authority, also carefully reviewed the manuscript and provided many constructive and valuable suggestions and helpful criticisms. This work would not have been written was it not for his encouragements and enthusiasm.

Of course, I am solely responsible for any error of theory or facts included herein.

REFERENCES

1. Bennett, K. (2008, May 23). Disappearance of the Aral Sea. Retrieved August 25, 2020, from http://www.wri.org/blog/2008/05/disappearance-aral-sea/
2. *China's Road to Disaster: Mao, Central Politicians and Provincial Leaders in the Unfolding of the Great Leap Forward 1955 – 1959*. Frederick C. Teiwes, Warren Sun. M E Sharpe, 1999. Routledge, 2015.
3. *Tombstone: The Great Chinese Famine 1958 – 1962*. Yang Jisheng. MacMillan Publishers, 2008.
4. *The Black Swan: The Impact of the Highly Improbable*. Nassim Nicholas Taleb. Random House, 2010.
5. *An Introduction to Complex Systems; Society, Ecology, and Nonlinear Dynamics*. Paul Fieguth. Springer, 2017.

6. *Complexity and the Economy*. W. Brian Arthur. Oxford University Press, 2015.
7. *Capital, Volume 1*. Karl Marx. Pelican Books 1976, Penguin Classics 1990.
8. *Imperialism, The Highest Stage of Capitalism*. Vladimir Ilyich Lenin, 1917
9. *Capital in the Twenty-First Century*. Thomas Piketty. The Belknap Press of Harvard University Press, 2014.
10. *After Piketty, the Agenda for Economics and Inequality*. H.Boushey, J. B. Delong, M. Steinbaum. Harvard University Press, 2017.
11. *The Soviet Century*. Moshe Lewin. Verso, 2005, 2016.
12. *The CIA World Factbook 2018-2019*. Central Intelligence Agency. Skyhorse Publishing, 2018.
13. Gun Owners of America. (2008, September 29). Fact Sheet: Guns Save Lives. Retrieved August 25, 2020, from http://gunowners.org/sk0802htm/
14. *The Federalist Papers*, Dover Thrift Editions (2014 edition), NO. 29: Concerning the Militia. Alexander Hamilton. 1788.
15. *The Constitution of the United States of America: Amendments to the Constitution of the United States of America*. Fall River Press, 2012 edition.
16. Finnegan, W. Venezuela, A Failing

State. (2016, November 4). Retrieved August 25, 2020, from http://www.newyorker.com/magazine/2016/11/14/venezuela-a-failing-state/

17. Coleman, C. (2018, April 6). What are your rights in tackling burglars? Retrieved August 25, 2020, from http://www.bbc.com/news/uk-43652308/

18. World Data Atlas, Rankings, Crime Statistics. Burglary rate (cases per 100,000 population). (n.d.). Retrieved August 25, 2020., from http://knoema.com/atlas/ranks/Burglary-rate/

19. GlobalEconomy.com. Theft rate - Country rankings. (n.d.). Retrieved August 25, 2020, from http://www.theglobaleconomy.com/rankings/theft/ (also includes homicide, kidnapping and robbery rates)

20. Peter G. Peterson Foundation (2020, July 14). How does the US healthcare system compare to other countries? Retrieved October 12, 2020, from http://www.pgpf.org/blog/2020/07/how-does-the-us-healthcare-system-compare-to-other-countries/

21. Axene, J. W. (2019, May 30). Take a number: Would long wait times in US healthcare be acceptable? Retrieved August 25, 2020, from http://stateofreform.com/news/2019/05/take-a-number-would-long-wait-times-in-us-healthcare-be-acceptable/

22. Scutti, S. CNN. (2018, April 26). British toddler Alfie Evans not allowed to leave country, UK court says. Retrieved August 25, 2020, from, http://www.cnn.com/2018/04/25/health/alfie-evans-appeal-bn/index.html
23. History.com Editors, (2019, June 6). Charlemagne. Retrieved August 25, 2020, from http://www.history.com/topics/middle-ages/charlemagne/
24. *Genghis Khan, his Conquests, his Empire, his Legacy*. Frank McLynn. Da Capo Press, 2015.
25. *A Concise History of Greece (Third Edition)*. Richard Clogg. Cambridge University Press, 2013.
26. *A Concise History of Italy (Second Edition)*. Christopher Duggan. Cambridge University Press, 2014.
27. *Charter Schools and Their Enemies*. Thomas Sowell. Basic Books, 2020
28. United Nations - Climate Change. The Paris Agreement. (n.d.). Retrieved August 25, 2020, from http://unfccc.int/process-and-meetings/the-paris-agreement/the-paris-agreement/
29. Moulds, J. World Economic Forum. These are the world's least – and most – corrupt countries. Retrieved August 25, 2020, from, http://www.weforum.org/agenda/2019/02/least-corrupt-countries-transparency-international-2018/

30. Corruption Around the World in 2019 - Transparency International – The Global Coalition Against Corruption (2019). Retrieved October 12, 2020, from http://www.transparency.org/en/cpi#
31. Ma, Q. (1998, March). National Aeronautics and Space Administration Goddard Institute for Space Studies. Greenhouse Gases: Refining the Role of Carbon Dioxide. Retrieved August 25, 2020, from http://www.giss.nasa.gov/research/briefs/ma_01/
32. *Global Warming & Climate Change Demystified*. Jerry Silver. The McGraw Hill Companies, Inc., 2008; graph page 14.
33. Investigators: Petit, J.F., et al. Carbon Dioxide Information Analysis Center. U.S. Department of Energy, Office of Science. (2012, December 5). Historical Isotopic Temperature Record from the Vostok Ice Core. Retrieved August 25, 2020, from http://cdiac.ess-dive.lbl.gov/trends/temp/vostok/jouz_tem.html
34. Jouzel, J., et al. (2007). Orbital and Millennial Antarctic Climate Variability over the Past 800,000 Years. Retrieved August 25, 2020, from http://www.jerome-chappellaz.com/files/publications/orbital-and-millennial-antarctic-climate-variability-over-the-past-800-000-years-85.pdf

35. *Plio-Pleistocene decline of African megaherbivores: No evidence for ancient hominin impacts.* J. Tyler Faith, John Rowan, Andrew Du, Paul L. Koch. Science, 2018; 362 (6417): 938 DOI: 10.1126/science.aau2728
36. Moore, P. (2016). The Positive Impact of Human CO_2 Emissions on the Survival of Life on Earth. Retrieved August 25, 2020, from http://fcpp.org/wp-content/uploads/2016/06/Moore-Positive-Impact-of-Human-CO_2-Emissions.pdf
37. Salla, M. (2018, June 28). More Scientists Confirm Volcanoes Rapidly Melting Antarctica's Ice Sheets. Retrieved August 25, 2020, from http://www.exopolitics.org/scientists-confirm-volcanoes-melting-antarcticas-ice-sheets/
38. *Tuberculosis in the Americas.* Pan American Health Organization. World Health Organization, Regional Office for the Americas. PAHO 2018.
39. *Critical Thinking, An Introduction to Reasoning.* Francis W. Dauer. Oxford University Press, 1989.
40. Kehrenbacher, K. (2015, August 27). Why the Solyndra mistake is still important to remember. Retrieved August 25, 2020, from http://fortune.com/2015/08/27/remember-solyndra-mistake/

41. *Clinton Cash*. Peter Schweizer. HarperCollins Publishers, 2015.
42. *Profiles in Corruption*. Peter Schweizer. HarperCollins Publishers, 2020.
43. *Capital and Ideology*. Thomas Piketty. Harvard University Press, 2020

www.ingramcontent.com/pod-product-compliance
Lightning Source LLC
Chambersburg PA
CBHW071126030426
42336CB00013BA/2213